SAN FRANCISCO
COOKING

Designed by Sally Strugnell
Recipe photography by Peter Barry
Recipes styled by Bridgeen Deery and Wendy Devenish
Introduction and captions by Ros Cocks
Edited by Jillian Stewart

CLB 2988
© 1993 Colour Library Books Ltd, Godalming, Surrey, England.
All rights reserved.
This 1993 edition published by Crescent Books,
Distributed by Outlet Book Company Inc., a Random House Company,
40 Engelhard Avenue, Avenel, New Jersey 07001.
Printed and bound in Singapore
ISBN 0 517 07297 1
8 7 6 5 4 3 2 1

SAN FRANCISCO COOKING

CRESCENT BOOKS
NEW YORK • AVENEL, NEW JERSEY

INTRODUCTION

The huge and accommodating bay, that was later to become San Francisco Bay, was discovered by the Spanish in 1769. But it was in 1848, when gold was first discovered in the surrounding hills, that a mass migration to San Francisco from all over the world began. So it was that just another American town with rather a nice bay turned overnight into an international mecca, which was to go on to foster an international cuisine to match.

The city grew on the proceeds of gold and by 1902 there was a population of over 400,000. The food in those days was pretty basic and dishes such as the Hangtown Fry – fried oysters, bacon and eggs – were the staple for the American nationals. Chinese were brought in to work the railroads, and a thriving Chinatown in one corner of San Francisco was fast emerging where solely Chinese food was eaten. Other significant enclaves in the city were Italian and French, each clinging to their own cuisines. In 1906 a devastating duo of earthquake and concomitant fire wreaked havoc in the boom city. In a way this did San Francisco a favor. The overcrowded, undisciplined gold mecca badly needed restructuring, and that is what it got. It became an elegant and gracious city as well as an important Pacific port and as such was a magnet for fashionable people with fashionable tastes. Nowadays, food has become a number one interest amongst the discerning population of San Francisco, due to the many different nationalities' cuisines knitted together within the city, and the excellent quality of the produce available.

It would be hard to list all the varieties of restaurant and culinary influence in San Francisco, but the most important in the culinary sense are probably Spanish, Mexican, Chinese, Italian and French. Strands of all these cuisines have been entwined and added to local foods to produce San Francisco's very own cuisine. The Spanish and Mexican tastes of tomatoes and peppers are cooked with local chicken and the myriad Pacific seafoods such as shrimp, swordfish, Dungeness crabs and oysters; noodles are cooked with Chinese mushrooms, fresh green broccoli and carrots and given oriental spice; seafood and crisp local vegetables are stir-fried in the Cantonese style; Italian pasta is dressed with snails and sun-dried tomatoes; and French fruity desserts are laced with Californian wines.

In San Francisco itself the climate is kind: warm, dry summers and mild, wet winters, similar to Europe's Mediterranean. Inland it is drier and hotter, but it is here that the Californians have pulled off a miracle with their once desert-like hinterland. In the San Joaquin Valley their wonderfully successful and varied fruit and vegetable crops are nurtured. Miles and miles of irrigation pipeline controlled by computers, and farmers dedicated to high-quality production, enable this phenomenal market garden to thrive. The season is long and colorful and it is no wonder that the locals have developed such an interest in fine foods when they have acres of peppers, tomatoes, melons, peaches, nectarines, grapes, figs, guavas, beans and nuts, to name but a few, growing right on their doorstep.

San Francisco cooking is all about realising the full potential of quality ingredients. Freshness is the leitmotif, whether its salads, fish, seafoods, meat, vegetables or fruit. Try these recipes, using the best ingredients, and you will discover that the San Franciscan taste for quality is infectious.

Right: the unusual beauty of Lombard Street is a double delight when the hydrangeas are in bloom.

Cioppino

Preparation Time: 40 minutes **Cooking Time:** about 40 minutes **Serves:** 6-8

California's famous and delicious fish stew is Italian in heritage; but a close relative of French Bouillabaisse, too.

Ingredients

1 lb spinach, well washed
1 tbsp each chopped fresh basil, thyme, rosemary and sage
2 tbsps chopped fresh marjoram
4 tbsps chopped parsley
1 large red pepper, finely chopped
2 cloves garlic, crushed
24 large fresh clams or 48 mussels, well scrubbed

1 large crab, cracked
1 lb monkfish
12 large shrimp, cooked and unpeeled
1 lb canned plum tomatoes and juice
2 tbsps tomato paste
4 tbsps olive oil
½-1 cup dry white wine
Pinch salt and pepper
Water

Chop the spinach leaves roughly after removing any tough stems. Combine the spinach with the herbs, red pepper and garlic, and set aside. Discard any clams or mussels with broken shells or ones that do not close when tapped. Place the clams or mussels in the bottom of a large pot and sprinkle a layer of the spinach mixture over them.

Prepare the crab as in recipe for Crab Louis, leaving the shells on the claws after cracking them slightly. Place the crab on top of the spinach and then add another spinach layer. Add the fish and a spinach layer, followed by the shrimp and any remaining spinach.

Mix the tomatoes, tomato paste, oil, wine and seasonings and pour over the seafood and spinach. Cover the pot and simmer the mixture for about 40 minutes. If more liquid is necessary, add water. Spoon into soup bowls, dividing the fish and shellfish evenly.

Avocado Soup

Preparation Time: 20-25 minutes plus 2 hours chilling time **Serves:** 4

Avocados are featured frequently in California cooking. A cold soup like this makes an easy summer meal.

Ingredients

2 large ripe avocados
1½ cups plain yogurt
2 cups chicken or vegetable stock
½ clove garlic, minced
Juice of 1 lemon

2 tsps chopped fresh oregano or
    1 tsp dried
Salt and white pepper
Chopped parsley to garnish

Cut the avocados in half lengthwise and twist to separate. Tap the stone sharply with a knife and twist to remove. Place the avocado halves cut side down on a flat surface. Score the skin with a sharp knife and then peel the strips of skin backwards to remove them.

　　Cut the avocado into pieces and place in a blender or food processor. Reserve 4 tbsps yogurt and add the remaining yogurt and other ingredients, except the parsley, to the avocado. Process until smooth and chill thoroughly. Pour the soup into bowls or a tureen and garnish with reserved yogurt. Sprinkle with parsley and serve chilled.

San Francisco's stunning skyline by night, taken from the city's Edith Coolbrith Park.

Napa Valley Artichokes

Preparation Time: about 30 minutes **Cooking Time:** 40 minutes **Serves:** 4

The Napa Valley is wine growing country, so white wine is a natural choice for cooking one of California's best-loved vegetables.

Ingredients

4 globe artichokes	4 black peppercorns
4 tbsps olive oil	2 lemon slices
1 clove garlic, left whole	1 cup dry white wine
1 small bay leaf	Pinch salt and pepper
1 sprig fresh rosemary	1 tbsp chopped parsley
2 parsley stalks	Lemon slices to garnish

Trim stems on the base of the artichokes so that they sit upright. Peel off any damaged bottom leaves. With scissors, trim the spiny tips off all the leaves. With a sharp knife, trim the top 1 inch off the artichokes with a sharp knife. Place the artichokes in a large, deep pan with all the ingredients except the chopped parsley, and lemon.

Cover the pan and cook for about 40 minutes, or until artichokes are tender and bottom leaves pull away easily. Drain upside down on paper towels.

Boil the cooking liquid to reduce slightly. Strain, add parsley and serve with the artichokes. Garnish with lemon slices.

Top: San Francisco's amazing and most distinctive building, the 853-foot Transamerica Pyramid, takes center stage in this view of downtown.

Tomato and Orange Salad with Mozzarella and Basil

Preparation Time: 20-25 minutes **Serves:** 4

Juicy tomatoes combine with mozzarella and basil in this classic Italian salad given Californian flair with bright oranges.

Ingredients

4 large tomatoes	4 tbsps olive oil
4 small oranges	1 tbsp balsamic vinegar
8 oz mozzarella cheese	Salt and pepper
8 fresh basil leaves	

Remove the cores from the tomatoes and cut into slices about ¼-inch thick. Cut a slice from the top and bottom of each orange and, using a serrated fruit knife, remove the peel in thin strips. Make sure to cut off all the white pith. Slice oranges into ¼-inch thick slices. Slice the mozzarella cheese into slices of the same thickness. Arrange the tomatoes, oranges and mozzarella in overlapping circles, alternating each ingredient. Use scissors to shred the basil leaves finely, and sprinkle over the salad. Mix the remaining ingredients together well and spoon over the salad. Chill briefly before serving.

The Japanese Tea Garden, in San Francisco's Golden Gate Park, was created in 1894 as a Japanese exhibit for the California Midwinter Exposition.

Californian Shrimp and Scallop Stir-Fry

Preparation Time: about 35 minutes **Cooking Time:** 8-10 minutes **Serves:** 4-6

Stir-frying came to California with Chinese settlers who worked on the railroads. It's the perfect way to cook seafood.

Ingredients

3 tbsps oil
4 tbsps pine nuts
1 lb uncooked shrimp, peeled
1 lb shelled scallops, quartered if large
2 tsps grated fresh ginger
1 small red or green chili pepper, seeded and finely chopped
2 cloves garlic, finely chopped
1 large red pepper, cut into 1 inch diagonal pieces
8 oz fresh spinach, stalks removed and leaves well washed and shredded
4 green onions, cut in ½ inch diagonal pieces
4 tbsps fish or chicken stock
4 tbsps light soy sauce
4 tbsps rice wine or dry sherry
1 tbsp cornstarch

Heat oil in a wok and add the pine nuts. Cook over low heat, stirring continuously until lightly browned. Remove with a slotted spoon and drain on paper towels. Add the shrimp and scallops to the oil remaining in the wok and stir over moderate heat until shellfish is beginning to look opaque and firm, and the shrimp look pink. Add the ginger, chili, garlic and red pepper and cook a few minutes over moderately high heat. Add the spinach and onion, and stir-fry briefly. Mix the remaining ingredients together and pour over the ingredients in the wok. Turn up the heat to bring the liquid quickly to a boil, stirring ingredients constantly. Once the liquid thickens and clears, stir in the pine nuts and serve immediately.

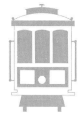

Spicy Oriental Noodles

Preparation Time: about 25 minutes **Cooking Time:** 7-8 minutes **Serves:** 4

A most versatile vegetable dish, this goes well with meat or stands alone for a vegetarian main course.

Ingredients

8 oz Chinese noodles (medium thickness)
5 tbsps oil
4 carrots, peeled
8 oz broccoli
12 Chinese mushrooms, soaked 30 minutes

1 clove garlic, peeled
4 green onions, diagonally sliced
1-2 tsps chili sauce, mild or hot
4 tbsps soy sauce
4 tbsps rice wine or dry sherry
2 tsps cornstarch

Cook noodles in boiling, salted water for about 4-5 minutes. Drain well, rinse under hot water to remove starch and drain again. Toss with about 1 tbsp of the oil to prevent sticking.

Using a large, sharp knife or Chinese cleaver, slice the carrots thinly on the diagonal. Cut the florets off the stems of the broccoli and divide into evenly-sized, but not too small sections. Slice the stalks thinly on the diagonal. If they seem tough, peel them before slicing. Place the vegetables in boiling water for about 2 minutes to blanch. Drain and rinse under cold water to stop the cooking, and let them drain dry.

Remove and discard the mushroom stems and slice the caps thinly. Set aside with the onions.

Heat a wok and add the remaining oil with the garlic clove. Leave the garlic in the pan while the oil heats and then remove it. Add the carrots and broccoli and stir-fry for about 1 minute. While continuously tossing the vegetables in the pan, add the mushrooms and onions and continue to stir-fry.

Combine the chili sauce, soy sauce, wine and cornstarch, mixing well. Pour over the vegetables and cook until the sauce clears. Toss with the noodles, heat them through and serve immediately.

Caesar Salad

Preparation Time: about 30 minutes **Cooking Time:** 3-5 minutes **Serves:** 4-6

This salad is said to have been concocted one evening from the only ingredients left in the kitchen.

Ingredients

6 anchovy fillets, soaked in
   4 tbsps milk
1 clove garlic
1 cup olive oil
4 slices French bread, cut into
   ½ inch cubes

1 egg, cooked 1 minute
Juice of 1 small lemon
Salt and pepper
1 head Romaine lettuce
4 tbsps grated Parmesan cheese

Soak the anchovies in the milk for 15 minutes. Rinse and pat dry on paper towels. Chop coarsely. Crush the garlic and leave in the oil for about 30 minutes. Heat all but 6 tbsps of the oil in a frying pan until hot. Fry the cubes of bread until golden brown, stirring constantly with a metal spoon for even browning. Drain on paper towels.

   Break the cooked egg into a bowl and beat well with the lemon juice, salt and pepper. Toss the lettuce with the remaining garlic oil and anchovies. Add the egg mixture and toss to coat well. Place in a serving bowl and sprinkle the croûtons and Parmesan cheese on top. Serve at room temperature.

Spanish influence is clear in these pleasing park buildings, and the towering palms give a clue to San Francisco's wonderfully benevolent climate.

Swordfish Florentine

Preparation Time: about 25 minutes **Cooking Time:** 6-8 minutes **Serves:** 4

Swordfish, with its dense texture, is a perfect and healthful substitute for meat. Here it has a distinctly Mediterranean flavor.

Ingredients

4 swordfish steaks about 6-8 oz
    each in weight
Salt, pepper and lemon juice

Olive oil
2 lbs fresh spinach, stems removed
    and leaves well wash

Aioli Sauce

2 egg yolks
1-2 cloves garlic
Salt, pepper and dry mustard

Pinch cayenne pepper
1 cup olive oil
Lemon juice or white wine vinegar

Sprinkle fish with pepper, lemon juice and olive oil. Place under a preheated broiler and cook for about 3-4 minutes per side. Fish may also be cooked on an outdoor barbeque grill.

Meanwhile, use a sharp knife to shred the spinach finely. Place in a large saucepan and add a pinch of salt. Cover and cook over moderate heat with only the water that clings to the leaves after washing. Do not add more water. Cook about 2 minutes, or until leaves are just slightly wilted. Set aside.

Place egg yolks in a food processor or blender. Add the garlic. Process several times to mix eggs and purée garlic. Add salt, pepper, mustard and cayenne pepper. With the machine running, pour oil through the funnel in a thin, steady stream.

When the sauce becomes very thick, add some lemon juice or vinegar in small quantities.

To serve, place a bed of spinach on a plate and top with the swordfish. Spoon some of the aioli sauce on top of the fish and serve the rest separately.

China Beach Salad

Preparation Time: about 30 minutes **Serves:** 4-6

Named for a stretch of beach near San Francisco, this recipe reflects the Chinese heritage in California's past and its present passion for salads.

Ingredients

1 lb cooked, peeled shrimp

1 lb seedless white grapes, halved if large

6 celery stalks, thinly sliced on the diagonal

4 oz toasted slivered almonds

4 oz canned water chestnuts, sliced or diced

8 oz canned lichees or 12 oz fresh lichees, peeled

1 small fresh pineapple, peeled, cored and cut into pieces

Dressing

1½ cups mayonnaise

1 tbsp honey

1 tbsp light soy sauce

2 tbsps mild curry powder

Juice of ½ a lime

Chinese cabbage or Belgian endive

Combine the shrimp, grapes, celery, almonds, water chestnuts and lichees in a large bowl. Trim off the top and bottom of the pineapple and quarter it. Slice off the points of each quarter to remove the core. Slice the pineapple skin away and cut the flesh into bite-size pieces. Add to the shrimp and toss to mix.

Break the Chinese cabbage or endive and wash them well. If using Chinese cabbage, finely shred the leafy part, saving the thicker ends of the leaves for other uses. Place the Chinese cabbage on salad plates. Mix the remaining dressing ingredients thoroughly. Pile the salad ingredients onto the leaves and spoon some of the dressing on top, leaving the ingredients showing. If using endive leaves, arrange them whole. Serve remaining dressing separately in a circle, radiating out from the salad.

Trout with Chorizo

Preparation Time: about 25 minutes **Cooking Time:** about 10 minutes for pre-cooking the sausages and 25 minutes for the fish **Serves:** 4

For fish with a spicy difference, try this as a dinner party dish to impress and please your fish-loving friends.

Ingredients

1 boned trout (about 2 lbs bone-in weight)
8 oz chorizo or other spicy sausage
Water
1 small green pepper, finely chopped
2 small onions, finely chopped
1 slice bread, made into crumbs

4 tbsps dry white wine
Lemon juice
½ cup plain yogurt
1 tsp garlic powder
2 tsps fresh coriander, chopped
Salt and pepper

Buy the fish cleaned, boned, but with the head and tail left on. Place the chorizo in a pan and cover with water. Bring to a boil and then cook for 10 minutes to soften and to remove excess fat. Skin sausage and chop it finely. Combine with the green pepper, onion, bread crumbs and wine. Sprinkle the fish cavity with the lemon juice.

Stuff the fish with the sausage mixture and place on lightly-oiled foil. Seal the ends to form a parcel and bake in a preheated 350°F oven for about 20-30 minutes, or until the fish feels firm and flesh looks opaque.

Combine the yogurt, garlic powder, coriander and seasonings to taste. Remove the fish from the foil and transfer to a serving plate. Spoon some of the sauce and over the fish and serve the rest separately.

San Francisco's Golden Gate Bridge, a tremendous feat of engineering, links the coastal highway south of San Francisco Bay to that lying north of the Bay.

Chicken Monterey

Preparation Time: 1 hour **Cooking Time:** 14-20 minutes **Serves:** 6

Accompanying this chicken recipe with colorful and spicy salsa gives it a touch of Mexican flavor.

Ingredients

6 boneless chicken breasts
Grated rind and juice of 1 lime
2 tbsps olive oil
Coarsely ground black pepper
6 tbsps whole grain mustard
2 tsps paprika
4 ripe tomatoes, peeled, seeded
  and quartered

2 shallots, chopped
1 clove garlic, crushed
½ Jalapeño pepper or other chili,
  seeded and chopped
1 tsp wine vinegar
Pinch salt
2 tbsps fresh coriander, chopped
Whole coriander leaves to garnish

Place chicken breasts in a shallow dish with the lime rind and juice, oil, pepper, mustard and paprika. Marinate for about 1 hour, turning occasionally.

To peel tomatoes easily, drop them into boiling water for about 5 seconds or less depending on ripeness. Place immediately in cold water. Peels should come off easily.

Place tomatoes, shallots, garlic, chili pepper, vinegar and salt in a food processor or blender and process until coarsely chopped. Stir in the coriander by hand. Set aside.

Place the chicken on a broiler pan and reserve the marinade. Broil chicken skin side uppermost for about 7-10 minutes, depending on how close the chicken is to the heat source. Baste frequently with the remaining marinade. Broil other side in the same way. Sprinkle with salt after broiling.

Place chicken on serving plate and garnish top with coriander leaves or sprigs. Serve with a spoonful of the tomato salsa on one side.

Fettucine Escargots with Leeks and Sun-Dried Tomatoes

Preparation Time: about 15-20 minutes   **Serves:** 4-6

These dried tomatoes keep for a long time and allow you to add a sunny taste to dishes whatever the time of year.

Ingredients

6 sun-dried tomatoes
14 oz canned escargots (snails), drained
12 oz fresh or dried whole-wheat fettucine (tagliatelle)
3 tbsps olive oil
2 clove garlic, crushed
1 large or 2 small leeks, trimmed, split, well washed and finely sliced

6 oyster, shittake or other large mushrooms
4 tbsps chicken or vegetable stock
3 tbsps dry white wine
6 tbsps heavy cream
2 tsps chopped fresh basil
2 tsps chopped fresh parsley
Salt and pepper

Chop the tomatoes coarsely. Drain the escargots well and dry with paper towels. Place the fettucine in boiling salted water and cook for about 10-12 minutes, or until al dente. Drain, rinse under hot water and leave in a colander to drain dry. Meanwhile, heat the olive oil in a frying pan and add the garlic and leeks. Cook slowly to soften slightly. Add the mushrooms and cook until the leeks are tender crisp. Remove to a plate. Add the drained escargots to the pan and cook over high heat for about 2 minutes, stirring constantly. Pour on the stock and wine and bring to a boil. Boil to reduce by about a quarter and add the cream and tomatoes. Bring to a boil then cook slowly for about 3 minutes. Add the herbs and salt and pepper to taste. Add the leeks, mushrooms and fettucine to the pan and heat through. Serve immediately.

Green Goddess Salad

Preparation Time: about 30 minutes **Serves:** 4

Named for its green dressing, this recipe combines Californians' love of fresh salads and avocados.

Ingredients

8 anchovy fillets, soaked in milk, rinsed and dried
1 green onion, chopped
2 tbsps chopped fresh tarragon or 1 tbsp dried
3 tbsps chopped fresh chives
4 tbsps chopped parsley
1 cup mayonnaise
½ cup plain yogurt
2 tbsps tarragon vinegar
Pinch sugar and cayenne pepper
1 large head lettuce
1 lb cooked chicken or seafood
1 avocado, peeled and cubed
1 tbsp lemon juice

Combine all the ingredients, except the lettuce, chicken or shellfish, avocado and lemon juice in a food processor. Work the ingredients until smooth, well mixed and green. Leave in the refrigerator for at least 1 hour for the flavors to blend.

Shred the lettuce or tear into bite-size pieces and arrange on plates. Top the lettuce with the cooked chicken cut into strips or cubes. If using seafood such as crab or lobster, cut the meat into bite-size pieces. Shelled shrimp or mussels can be left whole. Spoon the dressing over the chicken or seafood. Brush the avocado slices or toss the cubes with lemon juice and use them to garnish the salad. Serve any remaining dressing separately.

Top: Fisherman's Wharf was established in the late 1800s. Visitors crowd to the area's fish restaurants, renowned for their crab and shrimp dishes.

Chicken Jubilee

Preparation Time: about 20 minutes **Serves:** 6

Californian cooks are creative trendsetters. Trust them to change a cherry dessert into a savory recipe for chicken.

Ingredients

Oil

6 boneless chicken breasts

1 sprig fresh rosemary or ¼ tsp dried

Grated rind and juice of half a lemon

1 cup dry red wine

Salt and pepper

1 lb canned or fresh black cherries, pitted

2 tsps cornstarch

6 tbsps brandy

Heat about 4 tbsps oil in a frying pan over moderate heat. Place the chicken breasts, skinned side down, in first. Cook until just lightly browned. Turn over and cook the second side for about 2 minutes. Remove any oil remaining in the pan and add the rosemary, lemon rind, wine, and salt and pepper. Bring to a boil and then lower the heat.

Add the cherries, draining well if canned. Cook, covered for 15 minutes, or until the chicken is tender. Remove the chicken and cherries and keep them warm. Discard the rosemary if using fresh.

Mix the cornstarch, lemon juice and some of the liquid from the cherries, if canned. Add several spoonfuls of the hot sauce to the cornstarch mixture. Return the mixture to the frying pan and bring to a boil, stirring constantly, until thickened and cleared.

Pour the brandy into a metal ladle or a small saucepan. Heat quickly and ignite with a match. Pour over the chicken and cherries, shaking the pan gently until the flames subside. Serve immediately.

Walnut Grove Salad

Preparation Time: 25-30 minutes **Serves:** 6

Walnuts are very popular in Californian cuisine. In this recipe they add their crunch to a colorful variation on coleslaw.

Ingredients

1 small head red cabbage
1 avocado, peeled and cubed
1 carrot, grated
4 green onions, shredded
1 cup chopped walnuts

6 tbsps oil
2 tbsps white wine vinegar
2 tsps dry mustard
Salt and pepper

Cut the cabbage in quarters and remove the core. Use a large knife to shred finely or use the thick slicing blade on a food processor.

Prepare the avocado as in the recipe for Avocado Soup and cut it into small cubes.

Combine the cabbage, avocado and carrot with the onions and walnuts in a large bowl. Mix the remaining ingredients together well and pour over the salad. Toss carefully to avoid breaking up the avocado. Chill before serving.

Bay Bridge connects San Francisco with Oakland, a thriving port on the east side of San Francisco Bay.

Crab Louis

Preparation Time: 30-40 minutes **Serves:** 4

This salad is legendary on Fisherman's Wharf in San Francisco. Once tasted, it is sure to become a favorite.

Ingredients
2 large cooked crabs
1 head iceberg lettuce
4 large tomatoes
4 hard-cooked eggs
1 cup mayonnaise
4 tbsps whipping cream

4 tbsps chili sauce or tomato chutney
½ green pepper, seeded and
    finely diced
3 green onions, finely chopped
Salt and pepper
16 black olives

To prepare the crabs, break off the claws and set them aside. Turn the crabs over and press up with thumbs to separate the body from the shell of each. Cut the body into quarters and use a skewer to pick out the white meat. Discard the stomach sac and the lungs (dead-man's fingers). Scrape out the brown meat from the shell to use, if desired. Crack the large claws and legs and remove the meat. Break into shreds, discarding any shell or cartilage. Combine all the the meat and set it aside.

    Shred the lettuce finely, quarter the tomatoes and chop the eggs. Combine the mayonnaise, cream, chili sauce or chutney, green pepper, green onions, and salt and pepper, and mix well. Arrange the shredded lettuce on serving plates and divide the crab meat evenly.

    Spoon some of the dressing over each serving of crab and sprinkle with the chopped egg. Garnish each serving with tomato wedges and olives and serve the remaining dressing separately.

Lamb Steaks Alphonso

Preparation Time: about 1 hour **Cooking Time:** 20 minutes **Serves:** 4

Eggplant is a very popular vegetable in California cooking. Its taste is perfect with lamb marinated with garlic and rosemary.

Ingredients

4 large or 8 small round bone lamb
  steaks
4 tbsps olive oil
1 clove garlic, crushed
1 sprig fresh rosemary
Black pepper
1 tbsp red wine vinegar
4 tbsps olive oil
1 large eggplant
Salt
1 small green pepper, cut into 1 inch
  pieces

1 small sweet red pepper cut into
  1 inch pieces
2 shallots, chopped
4 tbsps olive oil
2 tsps chopped parsley
2 tsps chopped fresh marjoram
  or 1 tsp dried
6 tbsps dry white wine
Salt and pepper

Place lamb in a shallow dish with the oil, garlic, rosemary, pepper and vinegar and turn frequently to marinate for 1 hour.

Cut the eggplant in half and score lightly. Sprinkle with salt and leave on paper towels for about 30 minutes. Rinse well and pat dry. Cut eggplant into 1 inch pieces. Heat more oil in a frying pan and add the eggplant. Cook, stirring frequently, over moderate heat until lightly browned. Add peppers, shallots and herbs, and cook another 5 minutes. Add the wine and bring to a boil. Cook quickly to reduce the wine. Set the mixture aside.

Meanwhile, place the lamb on a broiler pan, reserving the marinade. Cook under a preheated broiler for 10 minutes per side. Baste frequently with the marinade. Serve the lamb with the eggplant accompaniment.

Tuna Baked in Parchment

Preparation Time: about 35 minutes **Cooking Time:** 10-12 minutes **Serves:** 4

This recipe uses a French technique called "en papillote." Californians, quick to spot a healthful cooking method, use it often with fish.

Ingredients

Oil
4 tuna steaks, about 8 oz each
  in weight
1 red onion, thinly sliced
1 beefsteak tomato, cut in 4 slices
1 green pepper, cut into thin rings
8 large, uncooked peeled shrimp

2 tsps finely chopped fresh oregano
  or 1 tsp dried
1 small green or red chili pepper,
  seeded and finely chopped
4 tbsps dry white wine or lemon juice
Salt

Lightly oil 4 oval pieces of wax paper about 8 x 10 inches. Place a tuna steak on half of each piece of paper and top with 2 slices of onion. Place a slice of tomato on each fish and top with green pepper rings. Place 2 shrimp on top and sprinkle over the oregano, salt and chili pepper.

Spoon the wine or lemon juice over each fish and fold the paper over the fish. Fold over the edges and pinch and fold to seal securely. Place the folded packets on a cookie sheet. Bake for about 10-12 minutes in a preheated 400°F oven. Unwrap each packet at the table to serve.

Above: San Francisco and the Bay Bridge beyond, which links the city to the communities on the east side of the Bay.

Zucchini Slippers

Preparation Time: 30 minutes **Cooking Time:** 23-25 minutes **Serves:** 6

Italian immigrants to California made the zucchini squash a popular food item in many delicious recipes.

Ingredients

6 evenly-sized zucchini
4 oz cottage cheese, drained
4 oz grated Colby cheese
1 small red pepper, seeded and chopped

2 tbsps chopped parsley
Pinch salt and cayenne pepper
1 large egg
Watercress or parsley to garnish

Trim the ends of the zucchini and cook in boiling, salted water for about 8 minutes, or steam for 10 minutes. Remove from the water or steamer and cut them in half. Allow to cool slightly and then scoop out the centers, leaving a narrow margin of flesh on the skin to form a shell. Invert each zucchini slipper onto a paper towel to drain, reserving the scooped-out flesh. Chop the flesh and mix with the remaining ingredients.

Spoon filling into the shells and arrange in a greased baking dish. Bake, uncovered, in a preheated 350°F oven for 15 minutes. Broil, if desired, to brown the top. Garnish with watercress or parsley.

There are estimated to be 75,000 Chinese in San Francisco's chinatown, concentrated in just a few city blocks around its main artery, Grant Avenue.

San Francisco Rice

Preparation Time: 25 minutes **Cooking Time:** about 20 minutes **Serves:** 4

This rice and pasta dish has been popular for a long time in San Francisco, where it was discovered.

Ingredients

4 oz uncooked long grain rice
4 oz uncooked spaghetti, broken
   into 2 inch pieces
3 tbsps oil
4 tbsps sesame seeds
2 tbsps chopped chives

Salt and pepper
1½ cups chicken, beef or
   vegetable stock
1 tbsp soy sauce
2 tbsps chopped fresh parsley

Rinse the rice and pasta to remove starch, and let drain dry. Heat the oil in a skillet and add the dried rice and pasta. Cook over moderate heat to brown the rice and pasta, stirring constantly. Add the sesame seeds and cook until the rice, pasta and seeds are golden brown. Add the chives, salt and pepper, and pour 1 cup of stock over the rice and pasta mixture. Stir in the soy sauce and bring to a boil.

Cover and cook about 20 minutes, or until the rice and pasta are tender and the stock is absorbed. Add more of the reserved stock as necessary. Do not let the rice and pasta dry out during cooking. Fluff up the grains of rice with a fork and sprinkle with parsley before serving.

A cablecar on California Street, center of the insurance business.

Vegetable Ribbons with Pesto

Preparation Time: 30-40 minutes **Cooking Time:** 45 minutes **Serves:** 4

There is no substitute for fresh basil in this sauce. Prepare it in the summer when basil is plentiful and freeze for later on.

Ingredients
2 large zucchini, ends trimmed
2 medium carrots, peeled
1 large or 2 small leeks, trimmed, halved and well washed
1 cup shelled pistachio nuts

2 small shallots, chopped
2-3 oz fresh basil leaves
1-1½ cups olive oil
Salt and pepper

Cut the zucchini and carrots into long, thin slices. Cut the leeks into lengths the same sizes as the zucchini and carrots. Make sure the leeks are well rinsed in between all layers. Cut into long, thin strips. Using a large, sharp knife, cut the zucchini and carrot into long, thin strips about the thickness of 2 matchsticks. Place the carrot strips in a pan of boiling, salted water and cook for about 3-4 minutes or until tender crisp. Drain and rinse under cold water. Cook the zucchini strips separately for about 2-3 minutes and add the leek strips during the last minute of cooking. Drain and rinse the vegetables and leave with the carrots to drain dry.

Place the nuts, shallots and basil in the bowl of a food processor or in a blender and chop finely. Reserve about 3 tbsps of the olive oil for later use.

With the machine running, pour the remaining oil through the funnel in a thin, steady stream. Use enough oil to bring the mixture to the consistency of mayonnaise. Add seasoning to taste.

Place reserved oil in a large pan and, when hot, add the drained vegetables. Season and toss over moderate heat until heated through. Add the pesto sauce and toss gently to coat the vegetables. Serve immediately.

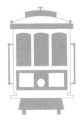

California Wild Rice Pilaff

Preparation Time: 25 minutes **Cooking Time:** about 20 minutes **Serves:** 4

Wild rice adds a nutty taste and a texture contrast to rice pilaff. It's good as a side dish or stuffing.

Ingredients

1 tbsp oil
1 tbsp butter or margarine
4 oz uncooked long-grain rice, rinsed
2 oz wild rice, rinsed
2 celery stalks, finely chopped

2 green onions
4 tbsps chopped walnuts or pecans
4 tbsps raisins
1½ cups chicken or vegetable stock

Heat the oil in a frying pan and drop in the butter. When foaming, add both types of rice. Cook until the white rice looks clear.

Add celery and chop the green onions, reserving the dark green tops to use as a garnish. Add the white part of the onions to the rice and celery and cook briefly to soften. Add the walnuts or pecans, raisins and stock. Bring to a boil, cover and cook until the rice absorbs the liquid and is tender. Sprinkle with the reserved chopped onion tops.

Alcatraz, an island in San Francisco Bay nicknamed The Rock, is famous for its federal penitentiary which was in use between 1933 and 1963.

Squash with Californian Blueberries

Preparation Time: about 30 minutes **Cooking Time:** 50-55 minutes **Serves:** 4

To steal the scene at any meal, serve this vegetable dish with simply cooked poultry or meat.

Ingredients
2 acorn squash

Freshly grated nutmeg

1 small apple, peeled and chopped

4 tbsps butter or margarine

4 tbsps light brown sugar

6 oz fresh or frozen blueberries

Cut the squash in half lengthwise. Scoop out the seeds and discard them. Fill the hollows with the chopped apple. Sprinkle on the sugar and nutmeg and dot with the butter or margarine.

Place the squash in a baking dish and pour in about 1 inch of water. Bake, covered, for 40-45 minutes at 375°F. Uncover, add the blueberries and cook for an additional 10 minutes.

Top: San Francisco's Victorian houses have been beautifully maintained and are highly prized properties.

Mango and Coconut with Lime Sabayon

Preparation Time: about 40 minutes **Cooking Time:** about 8 minutes **Serves:** 4

The taste of mango with lime is sensational, especially when served with the deliciously creamy sauce in this stylish dessert.

Ingredients

2 large, ripe mangoes, peeled
    and sliced
1 fresh coconut
2 egg yolks

4 tbsps sugar
Juice and grated rind of 2 limes
½ cup heavy cream, whipped

Arrange thin slices of mango on plates. Break coconut in half and then into smaller sections. Grate the white pulp, taking care to avoid grating the brown skin. Use the coarse side of the grater to make shreds and scatter them over the mango slices. Place egg yolks and sugar in the top of a double boiler or a large bowl. Whip until very thick and lemon colored. Stir in the lime juice and place mixture over simmering water. Whip constantly while the mixture gently cooks and become thick and creamy. Remove from the heat and place in another bowl of iced water to cool quickly. Whip the mixture while it cools. Fold in the whipped cream and spoon onto the fruit. Garnish with the grated lime rind.

Fisherman's Wharf was originally a thriving Italian enclave in San Francisco. Today, it is fashionable fish restaurants that abound.

Persimmon Pudding

Preparation Time: about 25 minutes **Cooking Time:** 45 minutes **Serves:** 6

This plump, bright orange fruit, spiced with preserved or fresh ginger, makes a rich and satisfying pudding for autumn.

Ingredients

2-4 ripe persimmons or Sharon fruit (depending on size)
4 tbsps honey
Juice and rind of 1 small orange
1 egg
½ cup light cream
¾ cup all-purpose flour
½ tsp baking powder
½ tsp baking soda
Pinch cinnamon and nutmeg
2 tbsps melted butter
1 small piece preserved ginger, finely chopped, or small piece freshly grated ginger

4 tbsps chopped walnuts or pecans
Whipping cream, orange segments and walnut or pecan halves to garnish

Orange Sauce
1 cup orange juice
Sugar to taste
1 tbsp cornstarch
2 tbsps brandy or orange liqueur

Peel the persimmons or Sharon fruit by dropping them into boiling water for about 5 seconds. Remove to a bowl of cold water and let stand briefly. This treatment makes the peels easier to remove. Scoop out any seeds and purée the fruit until smooth. Add the honey, orange juice and rind, egg and cream, and process once or twice. Pour the mixture into a bowl.

Sift the flour, baking powder, baking soda and spices over the persimmon purée and gradually fold together. Stir in the melted butter, ginger and nuts and spoon into well-buttered custard cups. Place in a bain marie and bake, in a preheated 350°F oven for about 45 minutes, or until risen and set. Test by inserting a skewer into the middle. If the skewer comes out clean the puddings are set. Allow to cool slightly. Combine the sauce ingredients and cook slowly, stirring continuously, until thickened and cleared. Stir in the brandy or orange liqueur. When the puddings have cooled slightly, loosen them from the edge of the dish and turn out onto a plate. Spoon some of the sauce over each and garnish with the cream, orange segments and nuts.

Striped Sorbet

Preparation Time: about 35 minutes plus 2 hours to freeze **Serves:** 4

A tricolored iced treat that can be prepared well ahead of time, this is a wonderful way to end a summer meal.

Ingredients
2 cups water
1 cup sugar
Juice of 1-2 lemons
8 kiwi fruit, peeled and coarsely
  chopped
4 ripe bananas, peeled and coarsely
  chopped

1 lb raspberries, fresh or well drained
  frozen
2 egg whites
1 banana, 1 kiwi fruit, sliced, and
  whole raspberries to garnish

Combine the water and sugar in a heavy-bottomed saucepan. Bring slowly to a boil to dissolve the sugar. When the sugar is completely dissolved, boil the syrup rapidly for about 1 minute. Allow it to cool completely and then refrigerate until completely cold. Purée the kiwi fruit in a food processor, sieving to remove the seeds if desired. Purée the bananas and the raspberries separately. Sieve the raspberries to remove the seeds. Divide the cold syrup in 3 parts and mix each with one of the fruit purees. Taste each and add about 1-2 tbsps of lemon juice to each fruit syrup, depending on the sweetness of the fruit. Freeze the fruit syrups separately until almost solid, about 2 hours, then mix again in the food processor to break up ice crystals. Freeze again separately until solid.

  Whip the egg whites until stiff. Process the sorbets again, separately, dividing the egg white among all three. Pour the raspberry sorbet into a bowl or mold and freeze until firm. Pour the banana sorbet on top and freeze again. Finish with the kiwi sorbet and freeze overnight or until firm. To unmold, dip briefly in hot water and invert on a plate. Garnish with the prepared fruit.

Pears in Zinfandel

Preparation Time: 25 minutes **Cooking Time:** about 50 minutes **Serves:** 6

Zinfandel has a spicy taste that complements pears beautifully. Add a garnish of crisp almonds for a Californian version of a French classic.

Ingredients

3 cups Zinfandel or other dry red wine
1 cup sugar
1 cinnamon stick
1 strip lemon peel
6 Bosc pears, evenly sized

4 tbsps sliced almonds
1 tbsp cornstarch mixed with
    3 tbsps water
Mint leaves to garnish

Pour the wine into a deep saucepan that will hold 6 pears standing upright. Add the sugar, cinnamon and lemon peel, and bring to a boil slowly to dissolve the sugar. Stir occasionally. Peel pears, remove "eye" on the bottom, but leave on the stems. Stand the pears close together in the wine, so that they remain standing. Cover the pan and poach gently over low heat for about 25-35 minutes, or until tender. If the wine does not cover the pears completely, baste the tops frequently as they cook.

Meanwhile, toast almonds on a cookie sheet in a moderate oven for about 8-10 minutes, stirring them occasionally for even browning. Remove and allow to cool.

When pears are cooked, remove from the liquid to a serving dish. Boil the liquid to reduce it by about half. If it is still too thin to coat the pears, thicken it with the cornstarch and water.

Pour syrup over the pears and sprinkle with almonds. Serve warm or refrigerate until lightly chilled. Garnish pears with mint leaves at the stems, just before serving.

Oranges in Red Wine

Preparation Time: about 40 minutes (syrup will take about 1 hour to cool completely) **Serves:** 4

Sunny California oranges look and taste beautiful in a rosy red sauce made with a good California red wine.

Ingredients
4 large oranges	6 tbsps water
1 cup sugar	½ cup full-bodied red wine

Using a swivel vegetable peeler, remove just the peel from the oranges. Be sure not to take off any white pith. Cut the peel into very thin strips. Peel off the pith from the oranges using small serrated knife. Take off the pith in thin strips to preserve the shape of the fruit. Peel the oranges over a bowl to catch any juice. Slice the fruit thinly and place in a bowl or on serving plates.

Place the sugar and water in a heavy-based saucepan over very low heat. Cook very slowly until the sugar dissolves completely and forms a thin syrup.

Add the strips of the peel and boil rapidly for 2 minutes. Do not allow the syrup to brown. Remove the peel with a slotted spoon and place on a lightly oiled plate to cool. Cool the syrup slightly and then pour in the wine. If the syrup hardens, heat very gently, stirring to dissolve again. Allow the syrup to cool completely. Spoon the syrup over the oranges and arrange the peel on top for serving.

San Francisco's magnificent City Hall was completed in 1915, a time of massive rebuilding, following the earthquake of 1906.

Flourless Chocolate Cake

Preparation Time: 15 minutes **Cooking Time:** about 1 hour **Serves:** 6

This is part mousse, part soufflé, part cake and completely heavenly! It's light but rich, and adored by chocolate lovers everywhere.

Ingredients

1 lb semi-sweet chocolate	6 tbsps sugar
2 tbsps strong coffee	1 cup whipping cream
2 tbsps brandy	Powdered sugar
6 eggs	Fresh whole strawberries

Melt the chocolate in the top of a double boiler. Stir in the coffee and brandy and let cool slightly.

Break the eggs into a bowl and then, using an electric mixer, gradually beat in the sugar until the mixture is thick and mousse-like. When the beaters are lifted the mixture should mound slightly.

Whip the cream until soft peaks form. Beat the chocolate until smooth and shiny, and gradually add the egg mixture to it. Fold in the cream and pour the cake mixture into a well greased 9-inch deep cake pan with a disk of wax paper in the bottom. Bake in a preheated 350°F oven in a bain marie. To make a bain marie, use a roasting pan and fill with warm water to come halfway up the side of the cake pan.

Bake about 1 hour and then turn off the oven, leaving the cake inside to stand for 15 minutes. Loosen the sides of the cake carefully from the pan and allow the cake to cool completely before turning it out.

Invert the cake onto a serving plate and carefully peel off the waxed paper. Place strips of wax paper on top of the cake, leaving even spaces in between the strips. Sprinkle the top with powdered sugar and carefully lift off the paper strips to form a striped or chequerboard decoration. Decorate with whole strawberries.

Hazelnut Florentines

Preparation Time: about 45-50 minutes **Cooking Time:** about 10 minutes per batch **Makes:** 24-30

Hazelnuts make a good alternative to almonds in these crisp, toffee-like cookies. They're a treat with coffee or ice cream.

Ingredients

1 lb shelled and peeled hazelnuts
1 cup sugar
6 tbsps honey
6 tbsps heavy cream

1 cup butter
6 oz white chocolate, melted
6 oz semi-sweet chocolate, melted

Place hazelnuts in a plastic bag and tie securely. Tap nuts or roll them with a rolling pin to crush roughly. Place sugar, honey, cream and butter in a heavy-bottomed saucepan and heat gently to dissolve sugar. Bring to a boil and cook rapidly for about 1½ minutes. Remove from heat and stir in the nuts.

Brush cookie sheets well with oil and spoon or pour out mixture in even amounts. Make only about six Florentines at a time. Bake for about 10 minutes in a preheated 375°F oven. Allow to cool on the cookie sheets and, when nearly set, loosen with a spatula and transfer to a flat surface to cool completely.

When all Florentines have been baked and cooled, melt both chocolates separately. Spread white chocolate on half of Florentines and semi-sweet chocolate on the other half, or marble the two if desired. Place chocolate side up to cool slightly and then make a wavy pattern with a fork, or swirl chocolate with a knife until it sets in the desired pattern.

Visitors soaking up the sights from San Francisco's magnificent natural harbor.

Appetizers:
Avocado Soup 12
Cioppino 10
Napa Valley Artichokes 14
Tomato and Orange Salad with Mozzarella and Basil 16
Californian Shrimp and Scallop Stir-Fry 18
Avocado Soup 12
Caesar Salad 22
California Wild Rice Pilaff 52
Californian Shrimp and Scallop Stir-Fry 18
Chicken Jubilee 36
Chicken Monterey 30
China Beach Salad 26
Cioppino 10
Crab Louis 40

Desserts:
Mango and Coconut with Lime Sabayon 56
Flourless Chocolate Cake 66
Hazelnut Florentines 68
Oranges in Red Wine 64
Pears in Zinfandel 62
Persimmon Pudding 58
Striped Sorbet 60
Fettucine Escargots with Leeks and Sun-Dried Tomatoes 32

Fish and Shellfish:
Crab Louis 40
Swordfish Florentine 24
Trout with Chorizo 28
Tuna Baked in Parchment 44
Flourless Chocolate Cake 66
Green Goddess Salad 34
Hazelnut Florentines 68
Lamb Steaks Alphonso 42
Mango and Coconut with Lime Sabayon 56

Meat:
Fettucine Escargots with Leeks and Sun-Dried Tomatoes 32
Lamb Steaks Alphonso 42
Napa Valley Artichokes 14
Oranges in Red Wine 64
Pears in Zinfandel 62
Persimmon Pudding 58

Poultry:
Chicken Jubilee 36
Chicken Monterey 30

Salads:
Caesar Salad 22
China Beach Salad 26
Green Goddess Salad 34
Walnut Grove Salad 38
San Francisco Rice 48
Spicy Oriental Noodles 20
Squash with Californian Blueberries 54
Striped Sorbet 60
Swordfish Florentine 24
Tomato and Orange Salad with Mozzarella and Basil 16
Trout with Chorizo 28
Tuna Baked in Parchment 44

Vegetable and Side Dishes:
Californian Wild Rice Pilaff 52
Squash with Californian Blueberries 54
San Francisco Rice 48
Spicy Oriental Noodles 20
Vegetable Ribbons with Pesto 50
Zucchini Slippers 46
Vegetable Ribbons with Pesto 50
Walnut Grove Salad 38
Zucchini Slippers 46